THE FOUNTAS AND PINNELL

Prompting Guide PART 1

A **Tool** for **Literacy** Teachers

Introduction

Readers and the Reading Process

Reading is a highly complex process. Each reader builds a system for processing texts that begins with early reading behaviors and becomes a network of strategic activities for reading increasingly challenging texts. The construction of the systems "in the head" is unique for each student. Marie Clay (1991) described readers' paths to proficient reading as "different paths to common outcomes."

You can observe the behaviors of readers as they process texts. From your observations, you infer the "in-the-head" actions (systems of strategic activities) a reader initiates to problem-solve getting the message of the text.

When readers process instructional level ["just-right"] texts, they engage their in-the-head systems and expand them as they problem-solve. They strengthen their reading power by putting their systems to work on the text.

Texts

Readers build processing systems by reading and writing connected text. To expand the system, the text needs to allow for a reader to do some problem solving against a backdrop of text that is read easily. The text needs to offer "just enough" challenge for the reader to "learn on the text."

When texts are arranged along a gradient from easy to more difficult, you can select a text that offers the right amount of challenge or opportunities for a reader to build his current strengths and support new learning. We have organized texts along an A to Z continuum to help you select appropriate texts for instruction.

Teaching

Your role is to notice each student's precise reading and writing behaviors and provide teaching that supports change in what she can do over time. As you infer from the behaviors how a reader or writer is building a system of strategic actions, you can make effective instructional decisions.

Observe accurate responses, partially correct responses, and incorrect responses so you can facilitate the student's problem solving by teaching for, prompting for, or reinforcing effective actions. The language in this guide is designed to help you initiate brief, powerful interactions that help readers build systems for working on print that readers can, over time, extend themselves (Clay, 1991).

Teaching for Strategic Actions in Reading and Writing

Reading

We suggest precise language for teaching so you can help readers use early behaviors and develop systems of strategic actions for processing texts.

EARLY READING BEHAVIORS Readers need to know where to look at and in what order to process the print as it is laid out on a page. This includes reading left to right and returning to the left to process a simple text. We include language designed to support the reader's ability to read left to right, return to the left, match one spoken word with one written word, and to check on himself.

SEARCHING FOR AND USING INFORMATION Readers need to learn how to look for and use the visual information, the language structure, and the meaning of the text as they problem-solve getting the message. They need to initiate attempts at problem solving, using all sources of information together.

SOLVING WORDS Readers need to learn how to analyze words. They need to develop a variety of flexible ways to use letter-sound relationships and word parts, so they can take words apart letter by letter or cluster by cluster or use what they know about words to help them read new words. They also need to learn how to use the language structure and the meaning of the text to support their word solving. When word solving is efficient and smooth, attention is freed for deeper thinking about the text.

MONITORING AND CORRECTING ERRORS Readers need to use all sources of information in the text to confirm their predictions or notice mismatches and work to correct them. Early readers display overt behaviors like stopping, hesitating, or making multiple attempts that indicate that they notice something is not right and they try to work it out. When efforts result in self-correction, the reader has engaged in important learning work. Self-correction changes over time, from rereading a whole sentence, to a phrase, to a correction at the word. Eventually it goes underground or "in the head." (Clay, 1991)

MAINTAINING FLUENCY Readers need to recognize words rapidly or take them apart quickly to read at a good rate. They need to anticipate language structure using phrase units, to vary their voice, stress the appropriate words, and read the punctuation. Effective readers use all of these characteristics in a smooth, integrated processing system.

Writing

We suggest language for the teaching of writing so you can help readers use early writing behaviors and strategic actions for composing and constructing words in texts. These basic competencies will support their independent writing.

COMPOSING SENTENCES Early writers need to learn how to compose language around a topic of interest. Engage the writer in thinking about ideas and communicating those ideas in language.

EARLY WRITING BEHAVIORS Writers need to learn how to place words on the page and form letters. They need to learn how to start on the left, move to the right, and return to the left to start again. They need to learn how to use the white space to differentiate words.

VERBAL PATH FOR LETTER FORMATION It is important to help students learn how to write letters efficiently so they can write with fluency. The specific language is used to get movement going in the right way. You can have the writer make the formations with a finger in the air, on the table, in sand or salt in a tray, or with a thick marker or thin marker to develop the movement early on. Over time, the actions become internalized and automatic and the language is not needed.

CONSTRUCTING WORDS Writers need to learn a variety of ways to construct words: through sound analysis, through visual analysis, and through the use of word parts and analogy. They also need to learn how to write high-frequency words quickly. It is also important that they learn how to monitor and correct their spelling.

CONVENTIONS Writers need to learn how to use capitalization and punctuation to convey accurate messages to readers. They need to reread their writing to check for conventions.

REVISITING THE TEXT FOR WORD STUDY Readers and writers need to confirm their knowledge of how words look. When they look back in the text, they consolidate their understandings of how words work. When writers revisit the written text, they learn how to notice aspects of words to support automaticity and fluency in reading and writing.

Using *Prompting Guide Part* ①

Prompting Guide Part 1 is designed to provide you with language and actions that support the reader's construction of an efficient network of strategic activities for processing texts and writing stories. The prompts provide short, explicit support for the student to engage in successful problem-solving actions and become independent in their use. Later, you may find that **General Problem-Solving** prompts (page 15) will help the student initiate problem-solving actions he has already learned. Over time, the overt behaviors will become unconscious and unseen.

Prompting Guide Part 1 is designed to support strategic activities within the text, while *Prompting Guide Part 2* is designed to provide you with language to support thinking beyond and about texts. The second tool will help you build your students' deep comprehension of a variety of text genres.

Your responses to the child's reading or writing may include:

TEACHING for Problem-Solving Actions

Demonstrate or model for the reader an explicit way to think about the text and/or tell the reader explicitly what to do.

PROMPTING for Problem-Solving Actions

Call for the student to think or act in a particular way with your actions or your language. The prompts provide a range of teacher support from very explicit to more general. They remind the reader to do what he has been taught to do to problem-solve. **For example**: *"Try that again"* is a very general prompt to be used only when you are certain that you have taught the student what to try, have evidence that the student understands what to do, and are confident that another attempt (search) will be successful.

REINFORCING Effective Problem-Solving Actions

Reinforce only newly emerging behaviors so they will become consistent. Your language confirms the reader's independent use of problem-solving actions.

Professional References

Clay, M. M. 1991. *Becoming Literate: The Construction of Inner Control.* Portsmouth, NH: Heinemann.

Clay, M. M. 2001. *Change Over Time in Children's Literacy.* Portsmouth, NH: Heinemann.

Fountas, I. C. and G. S. Pinnell. 1996. *Guided Reading: Good First Teaching for All Students.* Portsmouth, NH: Heinemann.

Fountas, I. C. and G. S. Pinnell. 2001. *Guiding Readers and Writers: Teaching Comprehension, Genre, and Content Literacy.* Portsmouth, NH: Heinemann.

Fountas, I. C. and G. S. Pinnell. 2006. *Teaching for Comprehending and Fluency: Thinking, Talking, and Writing about Reading, K–8.* Portsmouth, NH: Heinemann.

Johnston, P. 2004. *Choice Words: How Our Language Affects Children's Learning.* York, ME: Stenhouse.

McCarrier, A., G. S. Pinnell, and I. C. Fountas. 2000. *Interactive Writing: How Language & Literacy Come Together, K–2.* Portsmouth, NH: Heinemann.

Pinnell, G. S. and I. C. Fountas,. 2008. *The Continuum of Literacy Learning, K–8: Behaviors and Understandings to Notice, Teach, and Support.* Portsmouth, NH: Heinemann.

Pinnell, G. S., and I. C. Fountas. 1998. *Word Matters: Teaching Phonics and Spelling in the Reading/Writing Classroom.* Portsmouth, NH: Heinemann.

Early Reading Behaviors

 The development of early reading behaviors is the foundation for the reader's development of all subsequent reading and writing strategies. Observe carefully how the reader integrates oral language with motor movement.

Reading Left to Right/Return to Left

 Use actions along with this language at first and then shift to nonverbal prompts.

TEACH

Start here and read this way.

When you finish here, go back here. (point)

Hold the book on the edges. (model)

Move your eyes this way. (point)

You can say it slowly and move your finger under the word. Then you can do it with just your eyes.

PROMPT

You hold the book on the edges.

Now go back here.

Move your eyes.

Read it with your eyes.

Say it slowly and move your finger under the word. Now do it just with your eyes.

REINFORCE

You know how to hold the book on the edges.

You read it with your eyes.

Establishing Voice-Print Match

TEACH

Look at how I point and read. I make it match.

I'll point over and you point under.

Watch how I point under each word. I make it match.

Watch me point. I make it match.

Look how I do it. I make it match.

This is how to do it. Make it match.

Do this. I make it match.

Watch me. I make it match.

Watch me hold the book with both hands and read it with my eyes.

You can read it with just your eyes.

PROMPT

Use your pointer and make them match.

Point to each word.

Read it with your finger.

Put your finger under each word.

Was your finger under the word?

Don't cover up the words with your finger.

Read this page (or this line) with your finger.

Try again with your finger.

Use your eyes (pull finger away).

Take your finger out and use your eyes.

Hold the book with your hands and read it with your eyes.

Read it with your eyes.

Make your eyes move forward.

REINFORCE

You pointed under each word.

You read it with your finger and made it match.

You didn't need to use your finger to make it match.

You held the book with your hands and read it with your eyes.

You made it match.

Yes, that matched.

You were using your eyes.

You read it with your eyes.

Monitoring Voice-Print Match

TEACH

If you run out of words, go back and make it match.

You ran out of words. Go back and make it match.

If you have too many words, go back and make it match.

You have too many words. Go back and make it match.

This is _____ (tell a high-frequency word). Now read it again and make it match.

PROMPT

Did you have enough (or too many) words?

Did you run out of words?

Go back and make it match.

Were there enough words?

Did it match?

Did you make it match?

Read that line (or page) again with your finger and make it match.

Can you make it match?

Try that again and make it match.

You can fix that.

Show me _____ (a high-frequency word) on this page.

Now read it and make it match.

REINFORCE

You made it match.

You had just enough words.

You read it with your finger and made it match.

You tried it again and you made it match.

Searching for and Using Information

 Observe closely which source(s) of information the reader is already using, and then prompt for the student to use the source of information that will help him solve the problem quickly.

Meaning

TEACH

The picture will help you think about this part of the story.

You can think about the story.

You can think about the story when you look at the pictures.

You said _____. That doesn't make sense.

You said _____. That doesn't make sense in the story.

You said _____. That doesn't go with this part of the story.

PROMPT

Can the picture help you think about this part of the story?

Think about what would make sense.

Try that again and think of what would make sense.

Try _____(insert correct response). Would that make sense?

Are you thinking about what will happen next?

Are you thinking about the story?

Think about the story.

Think about what you know about this character (this story, this subject).

Think about who is talking now.

(Remind the student of the story context or meaning so far, e.g., "And then what did he do?")

REINFORCE

That makes sense.

That makes sense in (or goes with) this part of the story.

You were thinking about the story.

You were thinking about who was talking.

You were thinking about what would make sense.

You were thinking about what you know.

Structure

TEACH

You said _____. That doesn't sound right.

You said _____. That's not the way the writer would say it in a book.

Listen to this. (Model two choices.) Which one sounds better?

You can think what would sound right.

PROMPT

You said _____. Does that sound right?

Would _____ (model correct structure) sound right?

Try that again and think what would sound right.

Try _____(insert correct structure). Would that sound right?

REINFORCE

You made it sound right. (after problem solving)

That's how it would sound.

Visual Information

TEACH

You can read it again and start the word. (model rereading and articulate the first sound)

You can get your mouth ready to start the tricky word. (model)

You can say it slowly like when you write it. (model)

You can think of a part you know. (model)

It sounds like that, but it looks different.

PROMPT

Get your mouth ready for the first sound.

Sound the first part and think about what the word could be.

Think about the first sound.

Say the first sound.

That sounds like the beginning of _____.

What sound does it make?

What letter do you see first?

Look at the first letter (part).

What do you expect to see at the beginning (middle, end)?

Do you think it looks like _____?

It looks like _____ (insert another word they know).

Think about how the word looks.

Try _____. Would that look right?

What would look right there?

Do you know a word that would fit the meaning and look like (start like, end like) _____?

Can you find ___? (a known or new word)

Do you know a word like that?

Do you know a word that starts (ends) like that?

Is that like any other words you know?

Look at the first part (…the middle part. … the last part).

Think about what you know that might help.

What do you know like that?

Do you see a part that can help?

Say it slowly like when you write it.

Run a finger under it while you say it slowly.

Look at all the letters.

You are nearly right. Add a letter (ending) to make it look right.

REINFORCE

You thought about the first sound and it helped you.

You read that again and started the tricky word.

You thought about what would look right.

You added a letter and now it looks right.

You thought of another word like that.

You thought of another word you know.

You used a part you knew.

You looked at all the letters.

You thought about a part you know.

Your goal is to help readers use all sources of information together as they read text. These prompts will support their integration of all kinds of information.

Multiple Sources of Information

TEACH

It has to make sense and sound right.

It has to make sense and look right.

It has to sound right and look right.

It has to look right and make sense.

Listen, ... (say whole sentence). It makes sense and looks right.

Listen, ... (say whole sentence). It makes sense and sounds right.

Listen, ... (say whole sentence). It makes sense, sounds right, and looks right.

It has to make sense, sound right, and look right.

PROMPT

Do you know a word that would make sense and look like (start like, end like) _____?

Think of what would make sense and check with the letters.

Does that make sense and look right?

Does that make sense and sound right?

Does that sound right and look right?

Does that sound right and make sense?

Does that look right and sound right?

Does that look right and make sense?

Try that again and make it sound right and look right.

Try that again and make it make sense and look right.

What would make sense, sound right, and look like that?

Think of what would make sense, sound right, and look right.

Read from the beginning and try it again.

REINFORCE

You made it look right and sound right.

You made it make sense and look right.

You made it make sense and sound right.

You made it make sense, look right, and sound right.

Now it all fits together.

You made it all fit together.

Solving Words

 Your modeling and prompting should work the reader's eyes from left to right across the word. None of these should be used to direct the reader's attention to the middle/end of a word first.

Word Beginnings

 The word analysis prompts are mainly used to help a reader problem-solve because she has stopped and is unable to proceed, or after the reading of the text so as not to interrupt the flow of the story causing meaning to be lost.

TEACH

Listen to how I start it.

Look at the beginning.

You can get your mouth ready to start it.

Look at how I cover the last part. (expose only the first letter)

That's like _____. (known word with same first sound)

You can look at the letter and say the first sound.

PROMPT

Listen to how I start it.

It starts like this _____. (say sound)

Say the first part.

Cover the last part of the word.

Get your mouth ready to start the word.

Start it.

Say the sound of this letter.

Say the first sound.

Say more.

Say this much. (show part by part)

It starts like this_____. (show letter or letters with finger)

It starts like _____. (known word)

Do you know a word that starts with those letters?

Would _____ start like that?

See this letter.

Look at this letter.

Look at the first letter and say the sound.

Think about the sound the first letter makes.

REINFORCE

You got your mouth ready to start the word.

You said the first sound and it helped you.

You noticed the first letter and made the sound.

Solving Words *(continued)*

Word Parts (letter or cluster of letters)

TEACH

You can say it slowly like when you write it.

You can say the first part.

You can look at the first part, the next part.

You can look at the first syllable.

You can look for a part you know.

You can cover the last part.

You can think of a word like that.

You can break the word.

You can use your finger to break the word.

You can look for a part that might help.

PROMPT

Say it slowly like when you write it.
Look through the word.

Say the first part. Now, say more.
Look at the first syllable.
Say the first part, the next part…
Cover the last part.
Cover the end.
Say the first part. Say more. Now say the ending.

Look at the middle of the word.
Look at this part (point to middle).

Look at the last part.
Do you know a word that ends with those letters?
Look at the ending of the word.

Does this help? (point to part)
That's like_____.
Did you notice_____?
Notice the syllables.
Look at the base word (or root word).
Look at the prefix, the suffix.

Is that word like another word you know?
Do you know a word like that?
Look for a part you know.
Look for a part that can help
You can read a word that starts with that part.
Do you see a part that might help?
Where can you break the word apart?
Use your finger to break the word.
Look for something you know.
What do you know that might help?

REINFORCE

You said it slowly like when you wrote it.

You said the first part.

You noticed the first syllable.

You looked for a part you know.

You looked at the ending.

You covered the last part.

You thought of a word like that.

You used your finger to break the word apart.

Teach the reader how to confirm predictions and notice mismatches in the information. Prompt for self-monitoring after successful as well as unsuccessful attempts.

Self-Monitoring

TEACH

That didn't make sense (sound or look right). You need to stop when it doesn't make sense (sound or look right).

Watch me check it. (Reread, run your finger left to right under the problem word, and say the word slowly.) Yes, that looks right (or No, that doesn't look right).

Watch me check it. (Reread using expression and intonation.) Yes, that makes sense in this story (or No, that doesn't make sense in this story).

Watch me check. (Reread using expression and intonation.) That sounds right (or No, that doesn't sound right).

It has to make sense and sound right.

PROMPT

Why did you stop? What did you notice?

What is wrong?

Were you right?

What could you check?

Find the part that is not quite right.

Where is the tricky part?

Check it. (demonstrate where to check)

Put your finger under the tricky part.

You made a mistake. Can you find it?

What letter would you expect to see first in ____?

Check the first part of the word. (middle part)

It starts like that. Now check the last part (or end).

What letter would you expect to see last in ____?

Did you notice _____? (point up mismatch.)

Could it be ...? (say the sentence with meaningful choices in whole sentence)

You said _____. Does that make sense?

You said _____. Does that sound right?

You said _____. Does that look right?

Does the word you said look like the word on the page?

It has to make sense and go with the letters.

It has to make sense and look right.

It has to sound right and look right.

Could it be _____. Check to see if that looks and sounds right.

See if you can find what is wrong?

How did you know you were right?

How did you know it was _____?

REINFORCE

You found out what was wrong all by yourself.

You found the tricky part all by yourself.

You checked that with your finger all by yourself. You knew something was wrong.

You knew something wasn't quite right.

You knew how to make it right.

Self-Correcting

 Teach the reader how to monitor and search for and use information so he can self-correct errors while reading. Successful correcting will occur when the reader has been taught to self-monitor and search for and use information.

TEACH

You can try it again and think what would look right. (model)

You can try it again and think what would make sense. (model)

You can try it again and think what would sound right. (model)

PROMPT

You are nearly right. Try that again and think: What would look right?

You are nearly right. Try that again and think: What would sound right?

You are nearly right. Try that again and think: What would make sense?

You're almost right. Try that again.

How did you know it was _____?

How did you know you were right?

You _____. (acknowledge reader's problem solving) And did you notice _____?

Something wasn't quite right. See if you can fix that.

What else can you try?

You can fix that.

Work some more on that.

Try that again.

REINFORCE

You noticed what was wrong.

You tried to work it out all by yourself.

You had trouble and you figured it out.

You noticed that it didn't make sense. (sound right, look right)

You fixed that.

You went back and fixed it up.

You knew something wasn't quite right.

General Problem-Solving

 Earlier modeling and prompting were explicit calls for problem-solving actions. You modeled and prompted to call for the reader to problem-solve in explicit ways. Call for the reader to initiate problem-solving actions already learned by using these prompts.

Initiating Problem-Solving Actions

TEACH

You can try it another way. (model)

This will help. (model)

You can read that again and try something else. (model)

PROMPT

Look carefully and think what you know.

Look for something that will help you.

Do you see something that might help?

Look for what you know.

Think about what you know that might help.

Think about what it could be.

Think about what you know.

What can you do?

What do you know that might help?

What can you do to help yourself?

How can you help yourself?

What could it be?

What do you already know?

Try it another way.

Try something.

You can try that again.

You can work that out.

You can try that another way.

Stop doing that. You can do this.

That won't help you. This will help you.

Try that again.
(Caution: "Try that again" is a prompt to be used only when you are certain that you have taught the student what to try, have evidence the student understands what to do, and are confident that another attempt (search) will be successful.)

REINFORCE

You worked hard on that. [reinforcing language]

You thought about what you knew.

You tried that again.

You tried another way.

You tried to work that out.

You thought what it could be.

You worked that out.

Maintaining Fluency

 Be sure to insist on phrased, fluent reading early in the text so the reader processes the whole text with a forward momentum, thinking about the meaning and language structure while reading the text.

Rate

TEACH

I am going to read this faster.

Listen to how I read this.
Listen to how I read this quickly.

PROMPT

Listen to me read fast. Can you read it like that?

Read these words quickly. (model)

Can you read this quickly? (model)

Read this part again, faster.

Move your eyes forward quickly so that you can read more words together. (This may be accompanied by pushing a card across the line of text.)

REINFORCE

You read it faster that time.

You read it quickly.

You read more words together.

Pausing

TEACH

Listen to me read this. Can you hear me take a little breath at the comma?

Listen to me read this. Can you hear my voice go up at the question mark?

Listen to me read this. Can you hear my voice go down at the period?

PROMPT

Make a full stop at the period.

Make your voice go down when you see the period.

Make your voice go up when you see the question mark.

Take a little (or short) pause when you see the comma (or dash).

Set off the parentheses by stopping before them and after them.

Read it again and read the punctuation.

Read the punctuation.

REINFORCE

You took a little breath.

You made a full stop.

You made your voice go down when you saw the period.

You made your voice go up when you saw the question mark.

Phrasing

TEACH

Read it like this. (model phrase units)

Read this much all together. (cover part of the print, exposing phrase unit)

You need to listen to how your reading sounds.

Listen to me read this part. Now read it just like I did.

Listen to how I put my words together.

Listen to how I put my words together so they almost touch each other.

PROMPT

Can you make it sound like this? (model)

Let's put _____ _____ together.

Read these words together. (indicate)

These words make sense together. Read them together.

Read it all. (expose words with your finger or a card)

Put your words together so it sounds like the way you talk.

Put your words together so it sounds like talking.

Make it sound like talking.

Try that again and put your words together.

Are you listening to how your reading sounds?

REINFORCE

You put your words together. You made it sound like talking.

You were listening to how your reading sounded.

You made your words almost touch each other that time.

You made it sound like talking.

Stress

TEACH

Listen to how I make my voice sound... (scared, excited, happy, etc.)

Listen to how this sounds. (model)

When you see this big (boldface) print, make this word sound important. (louder)

When you see words in capital letters, make these words sound important.

PROMPT

Try that again and make that word sound important.

Try that again and say the dark word louder.

REINFORCE

You made that word sound important.

You made the dark word louder that time.

Intonation

TEACH

Listen to me read this. Can you hear my voice go down at the end?

Listen to me read this. Can you hear my voice go up at the question mark?

Listen to me read this. Can you hear how excited my voice sounds?

Listen to me read this. Can you hear how I sound like the characters who are talking?

PROMPT

Make your voice go down when you see the period.

Make your voice go down at the period. Then stop.

Make your voice go down at the period.

Make your voice go up when you see the question mark.

In this part, the _____ is asking a question. How would _____ ask the question?

Use emphasis when you see the exclamation point.

Make your voice show excitement when you see the exclamation point.

Make your voice sound like the character is talking when you see the speech marks (talking marks, quotation marks).

Make it sound like the characters are talking.

Make your voice sound like the character is talking.

In this part, _____ is very excited. How would _____ say that?

Take a short breath when you see the comma (or a dash).

Set off the parentheses by stopping before and after them.

Read the punctuation.

Change your voice when you see the _____ mark.

Are you listening to yourself?

Did it sound good?

Make it sound like a story you listen to.

Make your voice show what you think the author meant.

Make your voice show that you understand what the author means.

REINFORCE

You made your voice go down (up).

You sounded excited when you read that part.

You read the punctuation.

You made it sound like the character(s) was talking.

You made that story (part) sound interesting.

Integration

TEACH

Listen to how I read this. Can you read it the same way?

Make your reading sound smooth like this. (model)

PROMPT

Read it all smoothly.

Make it sound smooth.

Make your reading sound interesting.

Read it like the author is telling the story.

Tell the story with your voice.

How do you think your reading sounds?

REINFORCE

You made your reading sound interesting that time.

You are reading it like you are telling a story.

You sounded smooth that time.

You made it sound smooth.

Composing Sentences

Telling About Ideas

Every sentence the writer offers is a new combination of words. Help the writer put words together to express his ideas.

TEACH

Model going from thoughts or ideas to language, e.g., "This is one way to say it."

You can think about how you want to say it.

Think about what you want to tell about that.

Talk about what you are thinking about that.

You can say it slowly and listen for all the words you want to write.

PROMPT

Talk more about that.

Can you say more about that?

How would they say that in the book?

What can you tell about that? (Write about that.)

And how would you tell about that?

What would you say?

What happens first? (…next? …last?)

How would the character say that?

How did the character feel?

What is the problem in the story?

How did the character solve the problem?

Say more.

Tell more about your thinking.

Tell what happened then.

What else do you want to tell about that?

REINFORCE

That is an interesting way to say it.

That sounds like _____. (the character)

That sounds exciting.

That sounds interesting.

You told all about your thinking.

Early Writing Behaviors

 Engage the writer in thinking about ideas and how to put them into language (composition). Then support the writer to construct the message. Help her learn a variety of ways to construct words and self-monitor writing.

Placing Words on the Page

TEACH

Start here.

Write here next.

Leave some space before you start the next word.

When you get to the end, start here again.

Put the next word here.

PROMPT

Leave space to help your reader.

Can you see the space?

Feel the space with your finger.

Show a place where you left good space.

REINFORCE

You left good space before you started your word.

Look at all the good spaces.

Put your finger on a place where you left good space.

Verbal Path for Letter Formation

The Formation of Letters

TEACH

Use this language to show how to start and form each letter. You may want to model it with a large formation at first and then move to standard size.

Listen to how I say words to help me. Say the words to help you make the letters.

PROMPT

Have the students say the language with you as they trace or write a letter.

You know how to start it.

Think about how to write it.

REINFORCE

Have the students make the letter without using the language.

You knew how to start it.

You knew how to write it.

LOWERCASE LETTER FORMATION

a — pull back, around, up, and down
b — pull down, up, around
c — pull back and around
d — pull back, around, up, and down
e — pull across, back, and around
f — pull back, down, and cross
g — pull back, around, up, down, and under
h — pull down, up, over, and down
i — pull down, dot
j — pull down, curve around, dot
k — pull down, pull in, pull out
l — pull down
m — pull down, up, over, down and up, over and down
n — pull down, up, over and down
o — pull back and around
p — pull down, up, and around
q — pull back, around, up, and down
r — pull down, up, and over
s — pull back, in, around, and back around
t — pull down and cross
u — pull down, around, up, and down
v — slant down, up
w — slant down, up, down, up
x — slant down, slant down
y — slant in, slant and down
z — across, slant down, across

UPPERCASE LETTER FORMATION

A — slant down, slant down, across
B — pull down, up, around and in, back and around
C — pull back and around
D — pull down, up, around
E — pull down, across, across, and across
F — pull down, across, across
G — pull back, around, across
H — pull down, pull down, across
I — pull down, across, across
J — pull down, curve around, across
K — pull down, slant in, slant out
L — pull down, across
M — pull down, slant down, slant down, pull down
N — pull down, slant down, pull up
O — pull back and around
P — pull down, up, and around
Q — pull back and around and cross
R — pull down, up, around, in, and slant down
S — pull back, in, around, down, and back around
T — pull down, across
U — pull down, around, up, and down
V — slant down, slant up
W — slant down up, down up
X — slant down, slant down
Y — slant in, slant, and down
Z — across, slant down, across

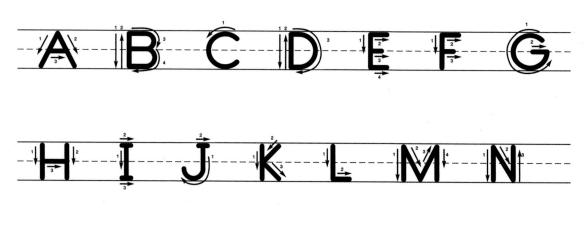

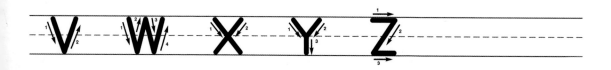

Constructing Words

Using Sound Analysis to Construct Words

TEACH

Model saying words slowly, listening for the sounds in sequence, and writing the letters that represent them.

You can say the word slowly and listen for the first, second, next, middle, last sound. (model)

You can say the word slowly and listen for the sounds.

You can think about each sound (first, middle, next, last) and write the letters. (model)

PROMPT

Listen for the parts.
Clap the parts you hear.

Listen for the sounds you hear in the first (last) part.
Listen for the consonant sound at the beginning (at the end, in the middle).
Listen for the vowel sound in the middle (at the beginning, at the end).
Listen for the ending (beginning, middle).
Listen for the first part (…the next part…. the last part).
Say the word aloud. Say it slowly.
Say the word slowly. What do you hear first? (next?)
Say the word slowly. How many sounds do you hear?

Write the letter for the first sound you hear, the next sound, the last sound.
What do you hear first? Next? At the end?
Did you write the letters for all the sounds you hear?

It sounds like _____. (another word they know)
It starts like _____. (use a known word)
It ends like _____. (use a known word)
Do you know another word that starts (ends) like that?
Do you know another word that sounds like that?
Is that like a word you know?
Do you know a word like that?
You can read a word that starts like that. (looks like)
Have you heard another word that starts like that? (sounds like that)
You can say another word like that.
Have you heard another word that sounds like that?
Have you heard another word that starts that way?
What letter do you expect to see at the beginning (or end)?
What's that like?

REINFORCE

You listened for the parts.
You said that word slowly.
You heard those sounds.
You heard all the sounds in order.
You heard the sounds and wrote the letters.

Using Visual Analysis to Construct Words

TEACH

Model writing using word parts, analogy, and thinking about orthographic (spelling) patterns to write unknown words as well as writing words quickly.

Add this to make it look right.

You know this word. (show)

You can think of a word you know. (model)

You know _____. Change the first letter(s), middle, end.

You can think about what looks right.

Watch me write this word fast.

Watch me write it like I know it.

Watch me write it without stopping.

PROMPT

It starts like _____. (ends like _____)

How do you think it would start? (end?)

Think carefully before you start.

Do you know a word that starts (ends) like that?

Do you know a word that starts with those letters?

You can read a word that looks like that. (starts, ends like that)

Look at the parts. (after the student has written a word)

Think about a part you know.

Write a part you know.

There's a silent letter at the beginning. (…at the end, next)

You need a vowel next in that word.

There are ____ letters.

Think of what the word means. Is it like another word you know?

It looks like ____ (another word they know).

Think of another word like that.

What's that like?

What do you know that might help?

It sounds like that, but it looks different.

What would make it look right?

Think about how the word looks.

You need to know that word. Do you have it in your head?

Write that quickly (or fast, without stopping).

Write it like you know it.

Do it faster.

Try it another time. (once more)

REINFORCE

You used a part you know.

You put a vowel in each part.

You added the ending.

You wrote all the letters.

You made it look right.

You made it like a word you know.

You wrote it fast.

You wrote it like you know it.

You wrote it without stopping.

Monitoring and Correcting Words

 Use actions along with this language at first, and then shift to nonverbal prompts.

TEACH

That part doesn't look right.

Let me show you how to check if all the sounds are there.

Let me show you how to check if all the letters are there.

Let me show you how to check the first part. (…the middle part. … the last part)

PROMPT

What did you notice? (after hesitation or stop)

What's wrong? Why did you stop?

Do you think it looks like _____?

Where's the tricky part? (after an error)

Find the part that's not quite right.

Does it look right?

Think about how the word looks.

How does it look?

What would make it look right?

What would look right there?

Check to see if all the sounds are there.

Check to see if that looks right.

Look closely at it and check it.

There's a tricky word on this line.

Something is not quite right.

You're almost right.

You're almost right. Add the ending.

You're nearly right. Change the middle.

You're nearly right. Add a letter to make it look right.

Try that another way.

Were you right?

REINFORCE

You checked all the sounds.

You checked all the letters.

You made it look right.

You worked that out all by yourself.

You noticed what was wrong.

You tried to work that out all by yourself.

You checked it carefully.

Conventions

Capitalization and Punctuation

TEACH

This is how to start the sentence. (show uppercase letters)

Start the sentence with an uppercase letter. (model)

This is how to end the sentence. It's a period. (model)

This is how to show excitement. It's an exclamation point. (model)

This is how to show it is a question. It's a question mark. (model)

This is how to show what the person is saying. These are speech marks (or quotation marks).

This is how to tell the reader to take a little breath.

PROMPT

Do you know how to start the sentence?

Think about how you always start the sentence.

Help your reader know where to stop.

Think about how to tell the reader where to stop.

Think about how to tell the reader to show excitement.

How can you show it is a question?

Show the reader you are asking a question.

How will you show what words _____ (the character) said?

Show where the talking starts and ends with speech marks.

Do you want to tell the reader to take a little breath there?

REINFORCE

You started the sentence with an uppercase letter.

You remembered to tell the reader where to stop.

You showed you were asking a question.

You showed where the talking started and where it ended.

You showed where to take a little breath.

Revisiting the Text for Word Study

 Use these prompts after the writing of any text to reinforce understandings about words and how they work.

Confirming Word Knowledge

TEACH

Model finding words and noticing different patterns or parts of words in a text.

PROMPT

Find a place where you used good spacing to divide the words.

Find the word _____.

Find a little word.

Find a big word.

Find the letter _____.

Find a word that begins with a capital letter.

Find a word that begins with a lowercase letter.

Find a word that begins with the two letters.

What word begins with (letter or letter cluster)?

What word begins like (word)?

What words begin with a consonant cluster? A vowel?

What word ends like (word)?

What's a word with two sounds (three, four, etc.)?

What word has more letters than sounds?

What words have one syllable (two, more than two, etc.)?

What word has parts that can be removed?

What words sound exactly like they look?

What words could be spelled another way but sound the same?

What words have a tricky (interesting, hard, new) pattern (spelling)?

What word has a special pattern (spelling) that shows what it means?

What word is a compound word (contraction, word with ending, word with prefix, etc.)?

What word is tricky (hard, new) for you to write? What will you want to remember about it?

What's a new word you learned how to write today?

REINFORCE

You knew how to find it quickly.

You checked your spaces.

You put good space between your words.

You found where the uppercase (lowercase) letter goes.

You learned a new word today.